BOB DYLAN COLLECTION

AMSCO PUBLICATIONS
NEW YORK/LONDON/SYDNEY

COVER PHOTOGRAPH LYNN GOLDSMITH/LGI
ARRANGEMENTS BY FRANK METIS
COMPILED BY LESLIE BARR WITH THANKS TO JEFF ROSEN

PUBLISHED BY AMSCO PUBLICATIONS,
A DIVISION OF MUSIC SALES CORPORATION, NEW YORK, NY.

ORDER NO. AM 80003
US INTERNATIONAL STANDARD BOOK NUMBER: 0.8256.1241.1
UK INTERNATIONAL STANDARD BOOK NUMBER: 0.7119.2314.0

EXCLUSIVE DISTRIBUTORS:
MUSIC SALES CORPORATION
225 PARK AVENUE SOUTH, NEW YORK, NY 10003 USA
MUSIC SALES LIMITED
8/9 FRITH STREET, LONDON W1V 5TZ ENGLAND
MUSIC SALES PTY. LIMITED
120 ROTHSCHILD STREET, ROSEBERY, SYDNEY, NSW 2018, AUSTRALIA

PRINTED IN THE UNITED STATES OF AMERICA BY
VICKS LITHOGRAPH AND PRINTING CORPORATION

BLOWIN' IN THE WIND

WORDS AND MUSIC BY BOB DYLAN

Moderately bright
D
G
A
D
G
D
mf
1. How many - y roads must a man walk down be - fore you call him a man? Yes, 'n' How man - y
2. How many - y times must a man look up be - fore he can see the sky? Yes, 'n' how man - y

G A D
seas must a white dove sail be - fore she
ears must one - man have be - fore he can
G A D
sleeps in the sand? Yes, 'n' how man - y
hear peo - ple cry? Yes, 'n' how man - y
G A D
times must the can-non - balls fly be - fore they're
deaths will it take 'til he knows and that too man - y
G D G
for - ev - er banned?
peo ple have died?
The an - swer, my

A
D
G
friend, is blow-in' in the wind, The an - swer is
A
D
1.2.
3.
blow-in' in the wind.

Additional Lyrics

3. How many years can a mountain exist
before it is washed to the sea?
Yes 'n' how many years can some people exist
before they're allowed to be free?
Yes 'n' how many times can a man turn his head
pretending that he just doesn't see?

The answer, my friend, is blowin' in the wind,
The answer is blowin' in the wind.

LAY, LADY, LAY

WORDS AND MUSIC BY BOB DYLAN

Slowly
A
5fr.
C#m/G#
4fr.
G
3fr.
Bm/F#
A
5fr.
C#m
4fr.
Lay, la - dy, lay,
lay a - cross my big brass bed.
G
3fr.
Bm
A
5fr.
C#m
4fr.
G
3fr.
Bm
A
5fr.
C#m
4fr.
Lay, la - dy, lay,
lay a - cross my big brass bed.
G
3fr.
Bm
E
F#m
A
5fr.
What - ev - er col - ors you have
in your mind,

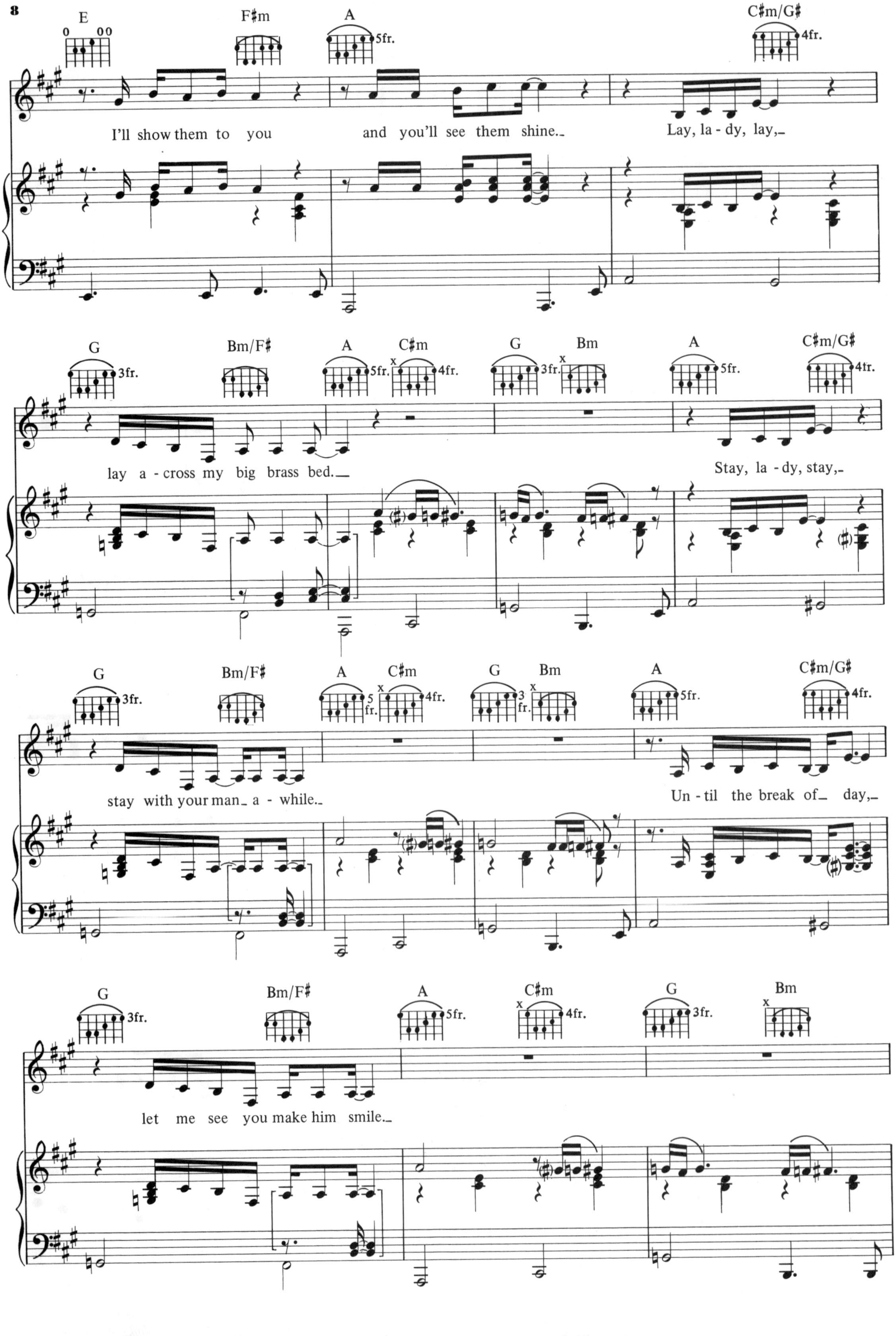
E F♯m A C♯m/G♯
I'll show them to you and you'll see them shine._ Lay, la - dy, lay,_
G Bm/F♯ A C♯m G Bm A C♯m/G♯
lay a - cross my big brass bed._ Stay, la - dy, stay,_
G Bm/F♯ A C♯m G Bm A C♯m/G♯
stay with your man_ a - while._ Un - til the break of_ day,_
G Bm/F♯ A C♯m G Bm
let me see you make him smile._

E
F♯m
A
5fr.
His clothes are dirt - y but his
hands are clean,
E
F♯m
A
5fr.
And you're the best thing that he's
ev - er seen.
C♯m/G♯
4fr.
G
3fr.
Bm/F♯
A
5fr.
C♯m
4fr.
Stay, la - dy, stay,
stay with your man a - while.
G
3fr.
Bm
C♯m
4fr.
E
F♯m
A
5fr.
Why wait an - y long - er for the world to be - gin,

C♯m
4fr.
Bm
A
5fr.
You can have your cake and eat it too.
C♯m
4fr.
E
F♯m
A
5fr.
Why wait an - y long - er for the one you love,
When he's stand - ing in front of you.
C♯m
4fr.
Bm
A
5fr.
C♯m
4fr.
3
Lay, la - dy, lay,
G
3fr.
Bm
A
5 fr.
C♯m
4fr.
G
3fr.
Bm
A
5fr.
C♯m
4fr.
lay a - cross my big brass bed.
Stay, la - dy, stay,

G Bm A C♯m G Bm
3fr. 5fr. 4fr. 3fr.
stay while the night is still a - head.
E F♯m A E F♯m
5fr.
I long to see you in the morn-ing light,
I long to reach for you
A C♯m/G♯ G Bm/F♯
5fr. 4fr. 3fr.
in the night.
Stay, la - dy, stay,
stay while the night is still a - head.
A C♯m G Bm A Bm C♯m D A
5fr. 4fr. 3fr. 5fr. 4fr. 5fr. 5fr.

IF NOT FOR YOU

WORDS AND MUSIC BY BOB DYLAN

Moderately bright
E
A
E
B
If not for you,
mf
A
E
B
A
Babe, I could-n't find the door,
Could-n't e-ven
E
B
A
G#m
4fr.
see the floor.
I'd be sad and blue,

F♯m7
E
B
A
If not for you.
E
B
A
E
B
If not for you,
A
E
A
Babe, I'd lay a-wake all night,
Wait for the
E
A
G♯m
4fr.
morn-in' light
to shine in through,

F♯m7 G♯m 4fr. F♯m7
But it would not be new,_ If not for you.
E A B E A
E B
If not for you, My sky would fall, Rain would gath-er
E A E
too._ With-out your love, I'd be no-where at all. I'd

F♯ B A G♯m F♯m
4fr.
be lost, if not for you, And you know it's true.
E A G♯m F♯m7 E
4fr.
A E
If not for you, My sky would fall,
B E A
Rain would gath - er too.
With-out your love, I'd

E
F♯
B
A
be no-where at all. Oh! What would I do, If not for you.
G♯m
F♯m
B
A
G♯m
F♯m7
B
A
G♯m
F♯m7
E
A
4fr.
E
A
If not for you, Win - ter would

E A E
have no spring, Could-n't hear the rob-in sing.
A G♯m F♯m7
I just would-n't have a clue. An-y-way it would-n't ring
G♯m F♯m7 B9sus4 E
true, If not for you.
A E
If not for you.
repeat and fade

I WANT YOU

WORDS AND MUSIC BY BOB DYLAN

Moderately bright (quasi in 2)
F
Verse:
1. The
mf
F
Am/E
guilt - y un - der - tak - er sighs, The lone - some or - gan
drunk - en pol - i - ti - cian leaps Up - on the street where
Dm
grind - er cries, The sil - ver sax - o - phones say I should
moth - ers weep, And the sav - iors who are fast a - sleep, They

C
Bb
re - fuse you. The cracked bells and
wait for you. And I wait for them to
C
washed - out horns Blow in - to my face with scorn, But it's
in - ter - rupt Me drink - in' from my bro - ken cup And
Dm
C
not that way, I was - n't born to lose you.
ask me to o - pen up the gate for you.
F
Chorus:
I want you, I

Am/E
Dm
want you,
I want you
C
so bad,
Hon-ey, I want
F
you.
1.
2. To Interlude
Fine
2. The
Now

Interlude:
Am
Dm
all my fa - thers, they've gone down,_ True love they've_ been with-
Am
Bb
out it. But all their daugh - ters put me down 'Cause I don't think a - bout_
C
_ it.
D.S.al Fine
(3rd and 4th Verses)
3. Well, I re -

Additional Lyrics

3. Well, I return to the Queen of Spades
And talk with my chambermaid.
She knows that I'm not afraid
To look at her.
She is good to me,
And there's nothing she doesn't see.
She knows where I'd like to be,
But it doesn't matter.
Chorus

4. Now your dancing child with his Chinese suit,
He spoke to me, I took his flute.
No, I wasn't very cute to him,
Was I?
But I did it, though, because he lied,
Because he took you for a ride,
And because time was on his side,
And because I ...
Chorus

ALL ALONG THE WATCHTOWER

WORDS AND MUSIC BY BOB DYLAN

Moderately, with a beat
Am Am/G F G Am Am/G
"There must be some way out of here," said the jok - er to the
mf
F G Am Am/G F G
thief, "There's too much con - fu - sion,
Am Am/G F G Am Am/G
I can't get no re - lief." "Busi - 'ness men, they

F G Am Am/G F G Am Am/G
drink my wine. Plow - men dig my earth, None of them a -
F G Am Am/G F G
long the line know what an - y of it is worth."
Am Am/G F G Am Am/G
"No rea - son to get ex - cit - ed," the thief, he kind - ly spoke,
F G Am Am/G F G
"There are man - y here a - mong us

Am Am/G F G Am Am/G
who feel that life is but a joke. But, you and I, we've
F G Am Am/G F G
been thru that, And this is not our fate,—
Am Am/G F G Am Am/G
So, let us not talk false - ly now, The hour is get - ting late."—
F G Am Am/G F G
— All a - long the watch tow - er,—

Am Am/G F G Am Am/G F G
Prin - ces kept the view,
While all the wom-en came and went,
Am Am/G F G Am Am/G F G
Bare - foot ser - vants, too.
Out - side in the dis - tance,
Am Am/G F G Am Am/G
A wild - cat did growl,
Two rid - ers were ap -
F G Am Am/G F G Am
proach - ing,
The wind be - gan to howl.

KNOCKIN' ON HEAVEN'S DOOR

WORDS AND MUSIC BY BOB DYLAN

Slowly
G
D
Am7
mp
Ma - ma, take this badge off of me,
Ma - ma, put my guns in the ground,
G
D
C
I can't use it an - y more.
I can't shoot them an - y more.
G
D
Am7
It's get - tin' dark, too dark for me to see,
That long black cloud is com - in' down,

G D C
I feel like I'm knock-in' on heav-en's door.
I feel like I'm knock-in' on heav-en's door.
G D Am7 G D C
Knock, knock, knock-in' on heav-en's door,
Knock, knock, knock-in' on heav-en's door,
G D Am7 G D
Knock, knock, knock-in' on heav-en's door,
Knock, knock, knock-in' on heav-en's door.
1. C
2. C
G D Am7
Repeat and fade
mp

SHELTER FROM THE STORM

WORDS AND MUSIC BY BOB DYLAN

Moderately, in 2
D
A
G
D
mf
D
A
G
1. 'Twas in an - oth - er life - time, one of toil and blood,
word was spoke be - tween us, there was lit - tle risk in - volved;
ly I turned a - round and she was stand - in' there
dep - u - ty walks on hard nails and the preach - er rides a mount;
lit - tle hill - top vil - age they gam - bled for my clothes;
D
A
when black - ness was a vir - tue and the
ev - 'ry - thing up to that point had been
with sil - ver brace - lets on her wrists and
but noth - ing real - ly mat - ters much, it's
I bar - gained for sal - va - tion an' they

G
x000
D
xx0
road was full of mud. I came in from' the wil -
left un - re - solved. Try im ag - in - ing a place
flow - ers in her hair. She walked up to me so grace -
doom a lone that counts. And the one-eyed un - der - tak -
gave me a le - thal dose. I of - fered up my in -
A
x0 0
G
x000
der - ness, a crea - ture void of form,
where it's al - ways safe and warm,
ful - ly and took my crowr. of thorns,
er, he blows a fu - tile horn,
no - cence and got re - paid with scorn,
"Come
D
xx0
D/A
x0
G
x000
D
xx0
in," she said, "I'll give you shel - ter from the storm."

A
G
D
And if I pass this way again you can rest assured I'll always do my best for her, on that I give my word.
I was burned out from exhaustion, buried in the hail, poisoned in the bushes and blown out on the trail.
Now there's a wall between us, somethin' there's been lost; I took too much for granted, got my signals crossed.
I've heard newborn babies wailin' like a mornin' dove, and old men with broken teeth stranded without love.
Well, I'm livin' in a foreign country, but I'm bound to cross the line; beauty walks a razor's edge, someday I'll make it mine.

D
A
In a world of steel - eyed death and men who are
Hunt - ed like a croc - o - dile,
Just to think that it all be - gan on a
Do I un - der - stand your ques - tion, man, is it
If I could on - ly turn back the clock to when
G
D
fight - ing to be warm.
rav - aged in the corn,
long for - got - ten morn,
hope - less and for - lorn?
God and her were born,
"Come in," she said, "I'll give
D/A
G
D
A
you shel - ter from the storm."
1.-4.
G
D
5.
G
D
2. Not a
3. Sud - den -
4. Well, the
5. In a
ritard.

TANGLED UP IN BLUE

WORDS AND MUSIC BY BOB DYLAN

Moderately, in 2
D
Dsus4 sus2
D
Dsus4 sus2
mf
D
C/D
D
1. Ear - ly one morn - in' the sun was shin - in', I was lay - in' in bed,
C/D
D
C/D
G
Won - d'rin' if she'd changed at all, If her hair was still

D
C/D
red. Her folks, they said our lives__ to - geth - er
D
C/D
D
Sure was gon - na be rough._ They nev - er did like__ Ma - ma's
C/D
G
home - made dress,_ Pa - pa's bank - book was - n't big e - nough. And
A
Bm
D
I was stand - in' on the side of the road,_ Rain fall - in' on my shoes.__

G
x000
A
x0 0
Bm
x
Heading out for the East Coast, Lord
D
xx0
G
x000
A
x0 0
knows I've paid some dues Get-tin' through.
C
x 0 0
G
x000
D
xx0
Dsus4 sus2
xx00 0
Tan-gled up in blue.
1.-6.
D
xx0
Dsus4 sus2
xx00 0
7.
C
x 0 0
G
x000
D
xx0

Additional Lyrics

2. She was married when we first met,
Soon to be divorced.
I helped her out of a jam, I guess,
But I used a little too much force.
We drove that car as far as we could,
Abandoned it out West.
Split up on a dark sad night,
Both agreeing it was best.
She turned around to look at me,
As I was walkin' away.
I heard her say over my shoulder,
"We'll meet again some day
on the avenue."
Tangled up in blue.

3. I had a job in the great north woods,
Working as a cook for a spell.
But I never did like it all that much,
And one day the axe just fell.
So I drifted down to New Orleans,
Where I happened to be employed.
Workin' for a while on a fishin' boat,
Right outside of Delacroix.
But all the while I was alone,
The past was close behind.
I seen a lot of women,
But she never escaped my mind,
And I just grew.
Tangled up in blue.

4. She was workin' in a topless place,
And I stopped in for a beer.
I just kept lookin' at the side of her face,
In the spotlight so clear.
And later on as the crowd thinned out,
I's just about to do the same.
She was standing there in back of my chair,
Said to me, "Don't I know your name?"
I muttered somethin' underneath my breath,
She studied the lines on my face.
I must admit I felt a little uneasy,
When she bent down to tie the laces
Of my shoe.
Tangled up in blue.

5. She lit a burner on the stove,
And offered me a pipe.
"I thought you'd never say hello," she said,
"You look like the silent type."
Then she opened up a book of poems,
And handed it to me.
Written by an Italian poet
From the thirteenth century.
And every one of them words rang true,
And glowed like burnin' coal.
Pourin' off of every page,
Like it was written in my soul
From me to you.
Tangled up in blue.

6. I lived with them on Montague Street,
In a basement down the stairs.
There was music in the cafes at night,
And revolution in the air.
Then he started into dealing with slaves,
And something inside of him died.
She had to sell everything she owned,
And froze up inside.
And when finally the bottom fell out,
I became withdrawn.
The only thing I knew how to do,
Was to keep on keepin' on,
Like a bird that flew.
Tangled up in blue.

7. So now I'm goin' back again,
I got to get to her somehow.
All the people we used to know,
They're an illusion to me now.
Some are mathematicians,
Some are carpenters' wives.
Don't know how it all got started,
I don't know what they're doin' with their lives.
But me, I'm still on the road,
Headin' for another joint.
We always did feel the same,
We just saw it from a different point
Of view.
Tangled up in blue.

WATCHING THE RIVER FLOW

WORDS AND MUSIC BY BOB DYLAN

Moderate blues
F
What's the mat - ter with me,___ I don't have
Wish I was back in the cit - y___ In - stead of this
mf
B♭7
much to say,__
old bank of sand,__ With the
F
G
Day - light sneak - in' through the win - dow And I'm still in this all -
sun beat - ing down o - ver the chim - ney tops_ And the one I love___ so close at

C
night ca - fe.
hand.
F
Walk - in' to and fro be - neath the moon Out to where the
If I had wings and I could fly,
B♭
trucks are roll - in' slow, To
I know where I would go. But

F
C7
sit down on this bank of sand And watch the
right now I'll just sit here so con-tent-ed-ly And watch the
F
F7/E♭
D°7
B♭m/D♭
1. F/C
N.C.
C7
2. F/C
N.C.
riv-er flow.
riv-er flow.
C7
Peo-ple dis-a-gree-ing on all just a-bout ev-ery-thing, yeah,
Peo-ple dis-a-gree-ing ev-ery-where you look,
mf
F
Makes you stop and all won-der why. Why
Makes you wan-na stop and read a book. Why

Dm
G7
on - ly yes - ter - day I saw some - bod - y on the street_ Who just_ could - n't help but
on - ly yes - ter - day I saw some - bod - y on the street_ That was_
C
C7
cry. Oh,_ this
real - ly shook._ But this
f
F
ol' riv - er keeps on roll - in', though, No
ol' riv - er keeps on roll - in', though, No

B♭7
mat - ter what gets in the way and which way the wind does blow, And as
mat - ter what gets in the way and which way the wind does blow, And as
F
C7
long as it does I'll just sit here And watch the
long as it does I'll just sit here And watch the
1.
F
F7/E♭
D°7
B♭m/D♭
F/C
N.C.
F
N.C.
riv - er flow.
2.
F
B♭7
riv - er flow.
Watch the

F
Bb7
riv - er flow,
Watch - in' the
riv - er flow,
Watch - in' the
riv - er flow.
But I'll sit down on this bank of
sand And watch the riv - er flow.
C7
N.C.
F7/A
Bb
Bbm
F7
molto ritard.

EVERYTHING IS BROKEN

WORDS AND MUSIC BY BOB DYLAN

Moderately, with a steady beat

E7
mf
Brok - en lines, broke - en strings, Brok - en threads,
A7
brok - en springs, Brok - en i - dols, brok - en heads,

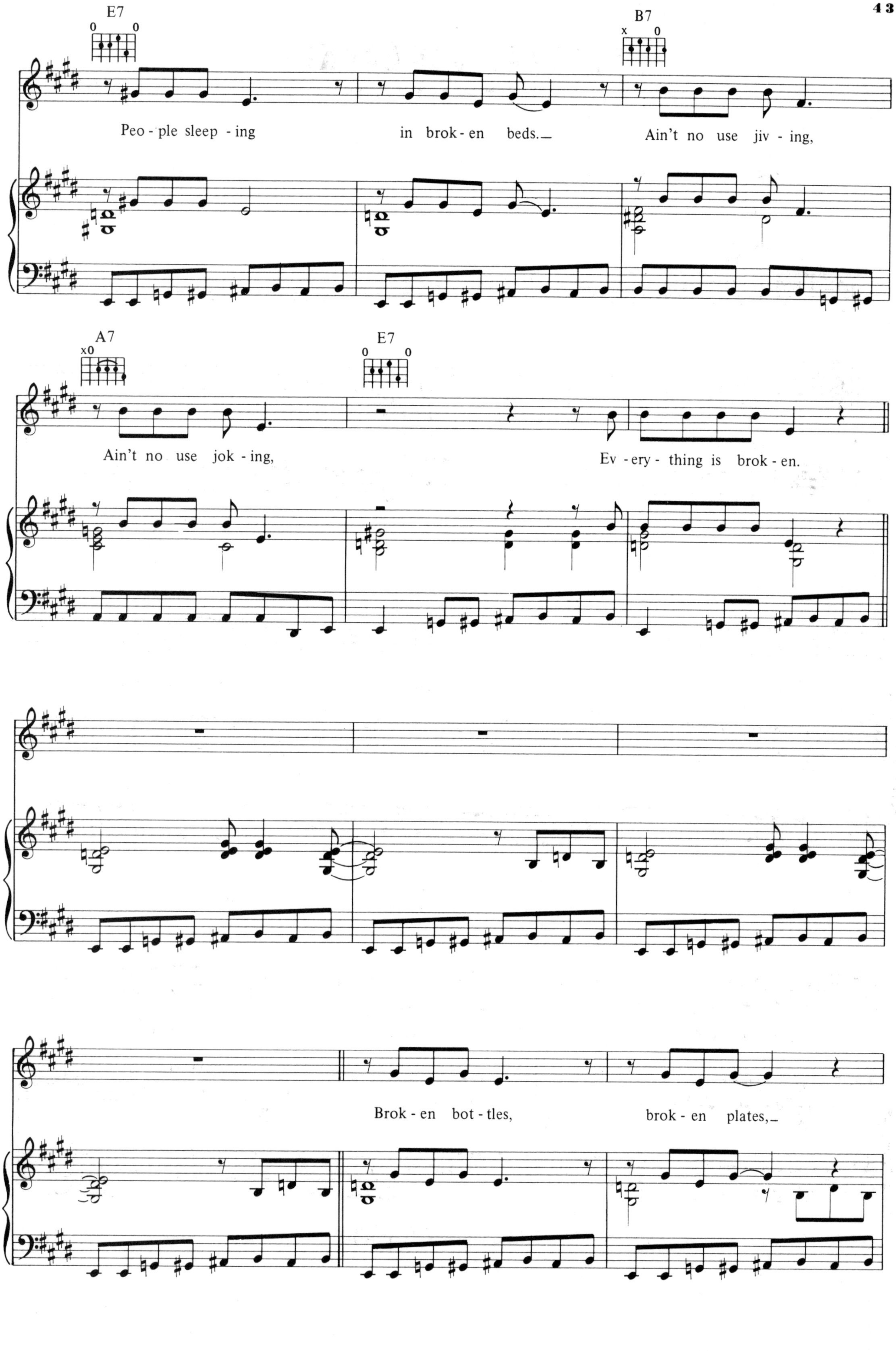
E7
B7
Peo - ple sleep - ing
in brok - en beds.
Ain't no use jiv - ing,
A7
E7
Ain't no use jok - ing,
Ev - ery - thing is brok - en.
Brok - en bot - tles,
brok - en plates,

A7
Brok - en switch - es,
brok - en gates,
Brok - en dish - es,
E7
brok - en parts,
Streets are filled
with brok - en hearts.
B7
A7
E7
Brok - en words
nev - er meant to be spok - en,
Ev -
ery - thing is brok - en.
f

B7
Seem like ev - ery time you stop and
A7
turn a - round,
Some - thing else just hit the ground.
E7
Brok - en cut - ters, brok - en saws,
Brok - en buck - les,
mf
A7
brok - en laws,
Brok - en bod - ies, brok - en bones,

E7
B7
Brok-en voic-es on brok-en phones. Take a deep breath,
A7
E7
feel like you're chok-in', Ev-ery-thing is brok-en.
E7
B7
Ev-ery time you leave and go off
f (opt. 2nd time)
mf
A7
some-place, Things fall to piec-es in my face.

E7
Brok-en hands_ on brok-en ploughs, Brok-en trea-ties,
A7
brok-en vows,_ Brok-en pipes,_ brok-en tools,_
E7
B7
Peo-ple bend-ing brok-en rules.___ Hound dog howl-ing,
A7
E7
bull-frog croak-ing, Ev - ery-thing is brok-en.
sfz

IDIOT WIND

WORDS AND MUSIC BY BOB DYLAN

Slowly, with a steady beat
Cm
D
1. Some-one's got it in__ for me, They're_plant - ing_ sto - ries_ in the_ press.
mf
G
Cm
Who - ev - er it is,__ I wish they'd cut it out But
D
G
when they will,________ I can on - ly guess.________ They

Em Bm Am G
say I shot a man named Gray, And took his wife to It-a-ly.
Em Bm Am G
She in-her-it-ed a mil-lion bucks, And when she died, it came to me. I can't
Bm C
help it if I'm luck-y.
Cm D
Peo-ple see me all the time, And they just can't re-mem-ber how to

G
Cm
act.
Their minds are filled with big i - deas,
D
G
im - ag - es and dis - tort - ed facts.
Em
Bm
Am
G
E - ven you, yes - ter - day, you had to ask me where it was at. I
Em
Bm
Am
G
could - n't be - lieve, af - ter all these years, you did - n't know me bet - ter than that,

Bm
C
sweet la - dy.
G
C
Id - i - ot wind,
blow - ing ev - ery time you move your
G
C
mouth,
Blow - ing down the back - roads head - in'
Dsus4
D
G
south.
Id - i - ot wind,

C
G
blow - ing ev - ery time you move your teeth.
You're an
C
D
id - i - ot, babe,
It's a won - der that you still know how to breathe.
1.-3.
G
C/G
G
C/G
4.
G
C/G
G
C/G
G

Additional Lyrics

2. I ran into the fortune teller, who said beware of lightning that might strike.
I haven't know peace and quiet for so long, I can't remember what it's like.
There's a lone soldier on the cross, smoke pourin' out of a boxcar door.
You didn't know it, you didn't think it could be done,
in the final end he won the war after losin' every battle.

I woke up on the roadside, daydreamin' 'bout the way things sometimes are.
Visions of you chestnut mare shoot through my head and are makin' me see stars.
You hurt the ones that I love best and cover up the truth with lies.
One day you'll be in the ditch, flies buzzin' around your eyes,
blood on your saddle.

Idiot wind, blowing through the flowers on your tomb,
Blowing through the curtains in your room.
Idiot wind, blowing every time you move your teeth.
You're an idiot, babe,
It's a wonder that you still know how to breathe.

3. It was gravity which pulled us down, and destiny which broke us apart.
You tamed the lion in my cage, but it just wasn't enough to change my heart.
Now everything's a little upside down,
as a matter of fact, what's bad is good.
You'll find out when you reach the top, you're on the bottom.

I noticed at the ceremony you corrupt ways had finally made you blind.
I can't remember your face anymore,
your mouth has changed, your eyes don't look into mine.
The priest wore black on the seventh day,
and sat stone-faced while the building burned.
I waited for you on the running boards near the cypress trees
while the springtime turned slowly into autumn.

Idiot wind, blowing like a circle around my skull,
From the Grand Coulee Dam to the Capitol.
Idiot wind, blowing every time you move your teeth.
You're an idiot, babe,
It's a wonder that you still know how to breathe.

4. I can't feel you anymore, I can't even touch the books you've read.
Every time I crawl past your door,
I been wishin' I was somebody else instead.
Down the highway, down the tracks, down the road to ecstasy,
I followed you beneath the stars,
hounded by your memory and all your ragin' glory.

I been doublecrossed now for the very last time,
and now I'm finally free.
I kissed goodbye the howling beast
on the borderline which separated you from me.
You'll never know the hurt I suffered not the pain I rise above.
And I'll never know the same about you, your holiness
or your kind of love,
And it makes me feel so sorry.

Idiot wind, blowing through the buttons of our coats,
Blowing through the letters that we wrote.
Idiot wind, blowing through the dust upon our shelves.
We're idiots, babe,
It's a wonder we can even feed ourselves.

POLITICAL WORLD

WORDS AND MUSIC BY BOB DYLAN

Brightly, with a driving beat (in4)

Gomit3rd
mf
1. We live in a po - lit - i - cal world,
Love don't have an - y place.
We're liv - ing in times where men com - mit crimes, And crime

1.
2.
don't have a face.
2. We
live in a po-lit-i-cal world,
I-ci-cles hang-ing down,
Wed-ding bells ring and an-gels sing,
Clouds cov-er up the ground.
3. We

live in a po-lit-i-cal world,_ Wis-dom is thrown in-to jail,_ It
rots in a cell, is mis-guid - ed as hell, Leav-ing no one to pick up a trail._
Gm
4. We
Gomit3rd
x00
live in a po-lit-i-cal world_ Where mer - cy walks the plank,_

Life is in mir-rors, death dis-ap-pears Up the steps in-to the near-est bank.
Gm
1.
2.
5. We
Gomit3rd
x00
live in a po-lit-i-cal world
Where cour-age is a thing of the past,
Hous-es are haunt-ed, chil-dren are un-want-ed, The next day could be your last.
6. We

live in a po-lit-i-cal world,
The one we can see and can feel.
But there's
no one to check, it's all a stacked deck,
We all know for sure that it's real.
Gm
7. We
Gomit3rd
x00
live in a po-lit-i-cal world,
In the cit-ies of lone-some fear.

Lit - tle by lit - tle you turn in the mid - dle, But you're nev - er sure why you're here.
8. We
live in a po - lit - i - cal world,
Un - der the mi - cro - scope,
You can
trav - el an - y - where and hang your - self there, You al - ways got more than e - nough rope.
Gm
9. We

Gomit3rd
live in a po-lit-i-cal world,_ Turn-ing and a-thrash-ing a-bout._ As
soon as you're a-wake, you're trained_ to take_ What looks like the eas-y way out._
Gm
10. We
Gomit3rd
live in a po-lit-i-cal world_ Where peace is not wel-come at all,_ It's turned a-

way from the door to wan-der some more Or put up a-gainst the wall. 11. We
live in a po-lit-i-cal world, Ev-ery-thing is hers or his,
Climb in-to the frame and shout God's name, But you're nev-er sure what it is.
Gm
Repeat and fade

NEVER GONNA BE THE SAME AGAIN

WORDS AND MUSIC BY BOB DYLAN

Moderately slow
Bb
Eb/Bb
Bb
Eb/Bb
mf
Bb
Eb/Bb
F
Now you're here be - side_ me, ba - by, you're a liv - ing dream. And
Sor - ry if I hurt you, ba - by, sor - ry if I did.
Bb
Eb/Bb
F
ev - ery time you get this close,_ it makes me want to scream. You
Sor - ry if I touched the place_ Where your se - crets are hid. But

Gb
Bb
Eb
touched me and you knew That I was warm for you and then,
you meant more than ev - ery - thing, and I could not pre - tend,
1.
Bb/F
F
Bb
Eb/Bb
I ain't nev-er gon-na be the same a-gain.
Bb
Eb/Bb
2.
Bb/F
Eb/F
I ain't nev-er gon-na be the same a-gain.

Bb
You
Gm
Cm
Bb
give me some-thing to think a-bout, ba - by, ev-ery time I see ya.
A
A7
Dm
Cm
F
Don't wor-ry, ba-by, I don't mind leav - ing, I'd just like it to be my i - de - a. You
Bb
Eb/Bb
F
taught me how to love you, ba - by, and you taught me, oh, so well. Now, I

B♭
E♭/B♭
F
can't go back to what was, ba - by, I can't un - ring the bell.
G♭
B♭
E♭
You took my re - al - i - ty and cast it to the wind And
B♭/F
F
B♭
E♭/B♭
I ain't nev-er gon-na be the same a - gain.
repeat and fade
B♭
E♭/B♭
B♭
E♭/B♭

Stuck Inside Of Mobile With The Memphis Blues Again

Words and Music by Bob Dylan

Moderately, with a beat
Verse:
F
Dm
F
1. Oh, the rag - man draws cir - cles Up and down the block.
mf
Dm
F
Dm
I'd ask him what the mat - ter was But I
Bb
C7
Bb
know that he don't talk. And the la - dies treat me kind -

F Dm F
- ly And fur-nish me with tape, But
Dm F Bb F
deep in - side my heart I know I can't es - cape.
Chorus:
Am
Oh, Ma - ma, can this real - ly be the end, To be stuck
F C/E Dm F/C C9sus4
1.- 8.
F
in - side of Mo - bile With the Mem - phis blues a - gain.
2. Well,
mf

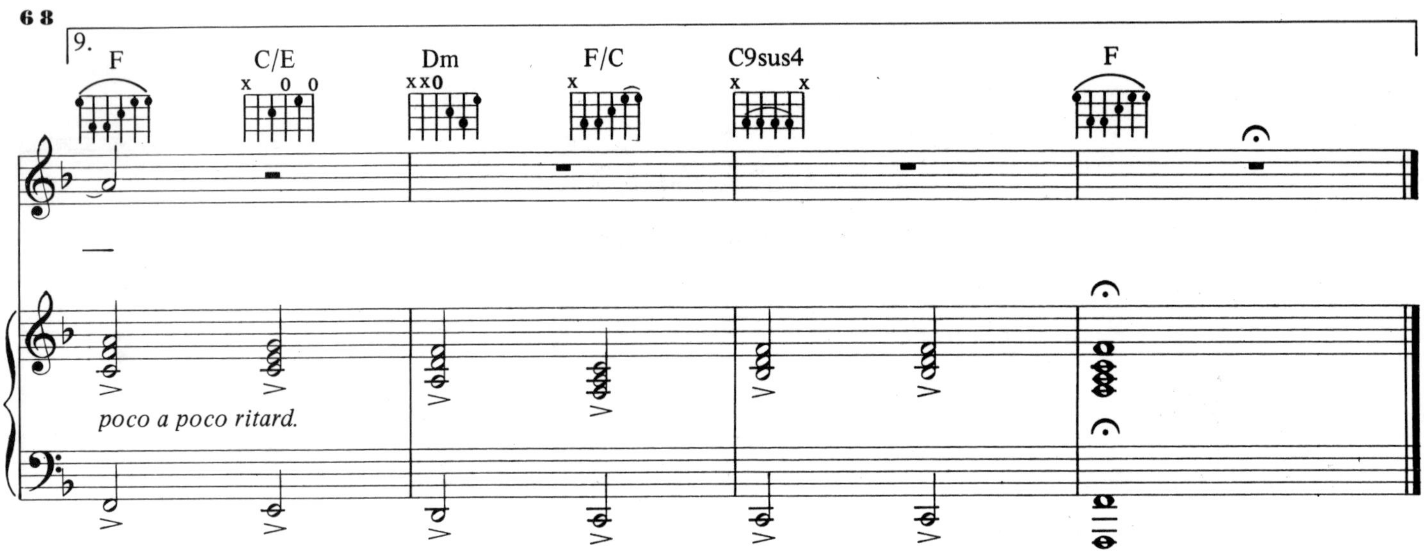
9.
F
C/E
Dm
F/C
C9sus4
F
poco a poco ritard.

Additional Lyrics

2. Well, Shakespeare, he's in the alley
With his pointed shoes and his bells,
Speaking to some French girl
Who says she knows me well.
And I would send a message
To find out if she's talked,
But the post office has been stolen
And the mailbox is locked.
Chorus

3. Mona tried to tell me
To stay away from the train line.
She said that all the railroad men
Just drink up your blood like wine.
An' I said, "Oh, I didn't know that,
But then again, there's only one I've met,
An' he just smoked my eyelids
An' punched my cigarette."
Chorus

4. Grandpa died last week
And now he's buried in the rocks,
But everybody still talks about
How badly they were shocked.
But me, I expected it to happen,
I knew he'd lost control
When he built a fire on Main Street
And shot it full of holes.
Chorus

5. Now the senator came down here
Showing ev'ryone his gun,
Handing out free tickets
To the wedding of his son.
An' me, I nearly got busted,
An' wouldn't it be my luck
To get caught without a ticket
And be discovered beneath a truck.
Chorus

6. Now the preacher looked so baffled
When I asked him why he dressed
With twenty pounds of headlines
Stapled to his chest.
But he cursed me when I proved it to him,
Then I whispered, "Not even you can hide.
You see, you're just like me,
I hope you're satisfied."
Chorus

7. Now the rainman gave me two cures,
Then he said, "Jump right in."
The one was Texas medicine,
The other was just railroad gin.
An' like a fool I mixed them,
An' it strangled up my mind.
An' now people just get uglier,
An' I have no sense of time.
Chorus

8. When Ruthie says come see her
In her honky-tonk lagoon,
Where I can watch her waltz for free
'Neath her Panamanian moon,
An' I say, "Aw come on now,
You must know about my debutante."
An' she says, "Your debutante just knows what you need,
But I know what you want."
Chorus

9. Now the bricks lay on Grand Street
Where the neon madmen climb.
They all fall there so perfectly,
It all seems so well timed.
An' here I sit so patiently,
Waiting to find out what price,
You have to pay to get out of
Going through all these things twice.
Chorus

I Shall Be Released

Words and Music by Bob Dylan

Moderately
A
Bm
1. They say ev - 'ry man must need pro - tec - tion,
mf
C♯m
E9sus4
A
D/A
They say ev - 'ry man must fall.
A
Yet I swear I see my re -

Bm
C♯m
4fr.
flec - tion
Some place
E9sus4
A
D/A
A
so high a - bove the wall.
Chorus:
Bm
I see my light come shin - ing
C♯m
4fr.
E9sus4
From the west down to the

A
east.
Any day now,
Bm
any day now,
C♯m
I
E9sus4
shall be re-
1,2. A
leased.
3. A
leased.
D/A
A
4fr.

Additional Lyrics

2. Down here next to me in this lonely crowd
   Is a man who swears he's not to blame.
   All day long I hear him cry so loud,
   Calling out that he's been framed.

   Chorus

3. They say ev'rything can be replaced,
   Yet ev'ry distance is not near.
   So I remember ev'ry face
   Of ev'ry man who put me here.

   Chorus

UP TO ME

WORDS AND MUSIC BY BOB DYLAN

Moderately, in 2
F
Am/E
B♭/D
1. Ev - ery - thing went from bad __ to worse, _ Mon - ey nev - er changed a thing, __
mf
Csus4
F
Am/C
B♭
__ Death kept fol - low - in', track - in' us down, At least I heard your blue - bird
Csus4
C
F
sing. Now some - bod - y's got to show their hand, time is an en - e - my, __

Bb
F
F/C
Bb
I know you're long gone, I guess it must be up to me.
1. - 11.
F
C
F
Bb
12.
F
2. If I'd

Additional Lyrics

2. If I'd thought about it I never would've done it,
   I guess I would've let it slide,
   If I'd lived my life by what others were thinkin',
   The heart inside me would've died.
   I was just too stubborn to ever be governed
   By enforced insanity,
   Someone had to reach for the risin' star,
   I guess it was up to me.

3. Oh, the Union Central is pullin' out
   And the orchids are in bloom,
   I've only got me one good shirt left
   And it smells of stale perfume.
   In fourteen months I've only smiled once
   And I didn't do it consciously,
   Somebody's got to find your trail,
   I guess it must be up to me.

4. It was like a revelation
   When you betrayed me with your touch,
   I'd just about convinced myself
   That nothin' had changed that much.
   The old Rounder in the iron mask
   Slipped me the master key,
   Somebody had to unlock your heart,
   He said it was up to me.

5. Well, I watched you slowly disappear
   Down into the officers' club,
   I would've followed you in the door
   But I didn't have a ticket stub.
   So I waited all night 'til the break of day,
   Hopin' one of us could get free,
   When the dawn came over the river bridge,
   I knew it was up to me.

6. Oh, the only decent thing I did
When I worked as a postal clerk
Was to haul your picture down off the wall
Near the cage where I used to work.
Was I a fool or not to try
To protect your identity?
You looked a little burned out, my friend,
I thought it might be up to me.

7. Well, I met somebody face to face
And I had to remove my hat,
She's everything I need and love
But I can't be swayed by that.
It frightens me, the awful truth
Of how sweet life can be,
But she ain't a-gonna make me move,
I guess it must be up to me.

8. We heard the Sermon on the Mount
And I knew it was too complex,
It didn't amount to anything more
Than what the broken glass reflects.
When you bite off more than you can chew
You pay the penalty,
Somebody's got to tell the tale,
I guess it must be up to me.

9. Well, Dupree came in pimpin' tonight
To the Thunderbird Cafe,
Crystal wanted to talk to him,
I had to look the other way.
Well, I just can't rest without you, love,
I need your company,
But you ain't a-gonna cross the line,
I guess it must be up to me.

10. There's a note left in the bottle,
You can give it to Estelle,
She's the one you been wondrin' about,
But there's really nothin' much to tell.
We both heard voices for awhile,
Now the rest is history,
Somebody's got to cry some tears,
I guess it must be up to me.

11. So go on, boys, and play your hands,
Life is a pantomime,
The ringleaders from the county seat
Say you don't have all that much time.
And the girl with me behind the shades,
She ain't my property,
One of us has got to hit the road,
I guess it must be up to me.

12. And if we never meet again,
Baby, remember me,
How my lone guitar played sweet for you
That old-time melody.
And the harmonica around my neck,
I blew it for you, free,
No one else could play that tune,
You know it was up to me.

LENNY BRUCE

WORDS AND MUSIC BY BOB DYLAN

Moderately slow, with expression

Ab Db Ab/C Ab Db Ab/C Eb/Bb Ebsus4
mp
Ab Db Ab/C Ab Db Ab/C Eb
1. Len - ny Bruce is dead but his ghost lives on and
Ab Eb Db Ab
on Nev - er did get an - y Gold - en Globe a - ward, nev - er

Db Ab/C Bbm Ab Eb Db
made it to Syn - a - non. He was an
Ab Db Ab Db
out - law, that's for sure, More of an out -
Ab Db Ab/C Bbm Ab Eb
law than you ev - er were.
Ab Db Ab/C Ab Db Ab/C Eb/Bb Db/Eb
Len - ny Bruce is gone but his spir - it's liv - in' on and

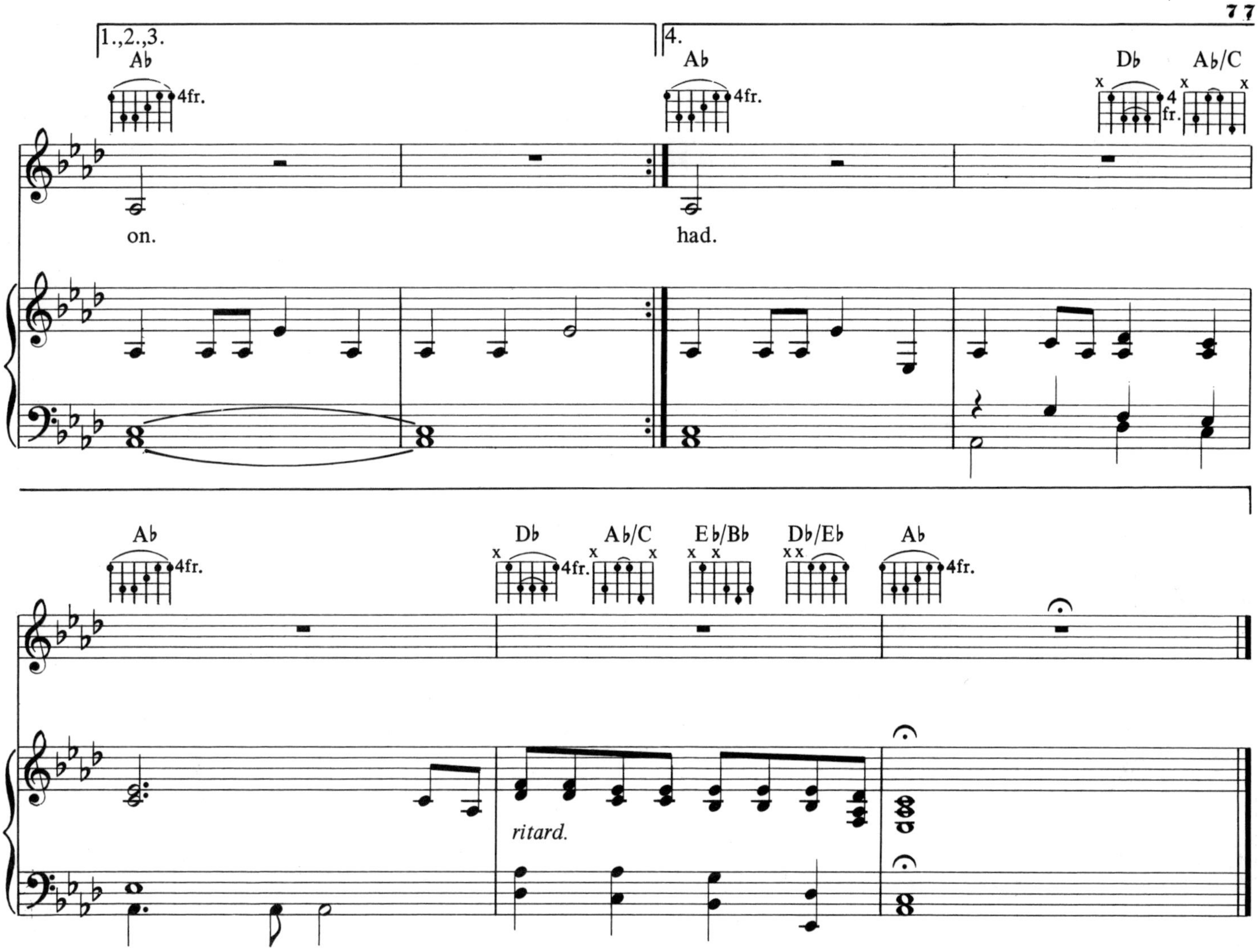
1.,2.,3.
Ab
4fr.
on.
4.
Ab
4fr.
had.
Db
Ab/C
4 fr.
Ab
4fr.
Db
4fr.
Ab/C
Eb/Bb
Db/Eb
Ab
4fr.
ritard.

Additional Lyrics

2. Maybe he had some problems, maybe some things that he couldn't work out
But he sure was funny and he sure told the truth and he knew what he was talkin' about.
Never robbed any churches nor cut off any babies'heads,
He just took the folks in high places and he shined a light in their beds.
He's on some other shore, He didn't wanna live anymore.

3. Lenny Bruce is dead but he didn't commit any crime
He just had the insight to rip off the lid before its time
I rode with him in a taxi once,
Only for a mile and half, Seemed like it took a couple of months.
Lenny Bruce moved on and like the ones that killed him, gone.

4. They said that he was sick 'cause he didn't play by the rules
He just showed the wise men of his day to be nothing more than fools.
They stamped him and they labeled him like they do with pants and shirts,
He fought a war on a battlefield where every victory hurts.
Lenny Bruce was bad, He was the brother that you never had.

ON A NIGHT LIKE THIS

WORDS AND MUSIC BY BOB DYLAN

Moderately bright, with a beat

C
G7
On a night like this So glad you came a - round,
So glad you've come to stay.
I can't get an - y sleep,
mf
C
Hold on to me so tight And heat up some cof - fee grounds.
Hold on to me, pret - ty miss Say you'll nev-er go a - way to stray.
The air is so cold out - side And the snow's so deep.
C7/E
F
We got much to talk a - bout And much to rem - i - nisce,
Run your fin - gers down my spine Bring me a touch of bliss
Build a fire, throw on logs And lis - ten to it hiss,

Dm7♭5
C
G7
C
1.,2.
It sure is right
On a night like this.
It sure feels right
On a night like this.
And let it burn,
burn, burn, burn
On a night like this.
N.C.
3. C
F
On a night like this,
On a night like this,
Put your bod - y next
C
to mine and keep me com - pa - ny,
D7
G7
N.C.
There is plen - ty a room for all, So please don't el - bow me.

C
G7
Let the four winds blow a - round this old cab - in door,
C
If I'm not too far off I think we did this once be - fore.
C7/E
F
There's more frost on the win - dow glass with each new ten - der kiss,
Dm7♭5
C
G7
C
But it sure feels right On a night like this.

LEOPARD SKIN PILLBOX HAT

WORDS AND MUSIC BY BOB DYLAN

E7
A
A7/C♯
C°7
E7/B
A
E7
1. Well, I
A
D7
see you got your
brand new leop-ard-skin pill - box hat

A
Yes, I
D7
see you got your brand new leop-ard-skin pill - box hat
A
Well, you must
E7
tell me, ba-by how your head feels un-der some-thin' like that

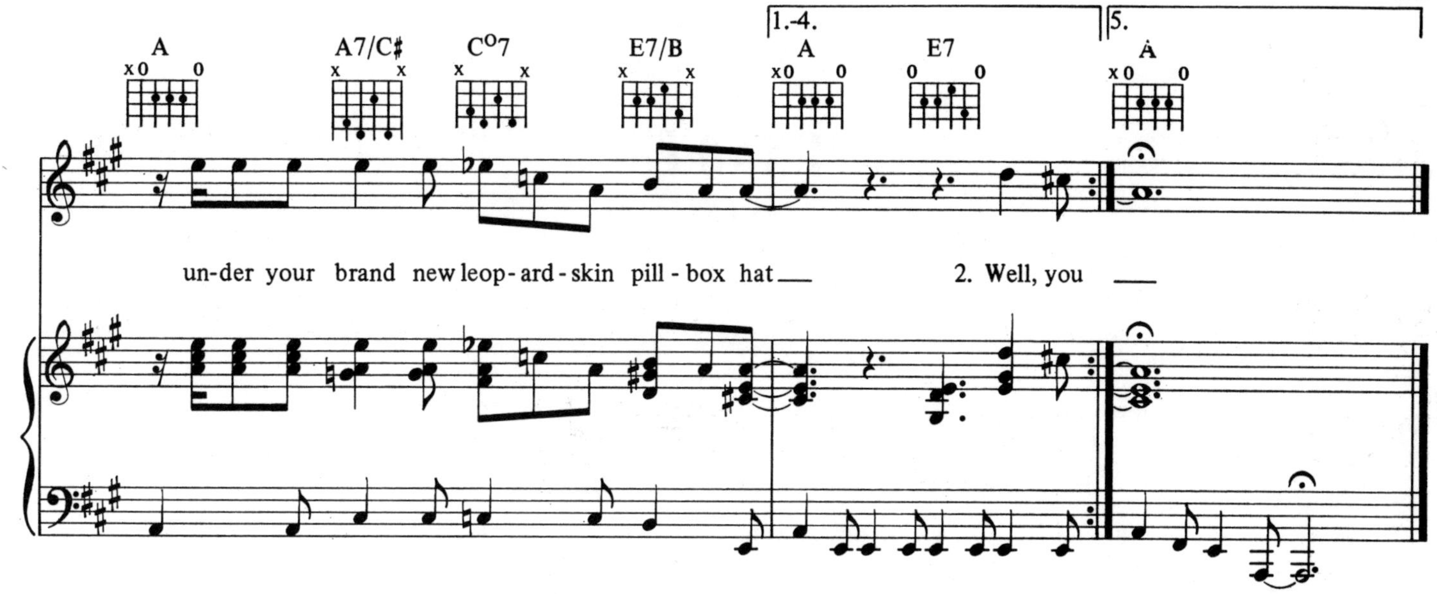
1.-4.
5.
A
A7/C♯
C°7
E7/B
A
E7
A
un-der your brand new leop-ard-skin pill-box hat
2. Well, you

Additional Lyrics

2. Well, you look so pretty in it
Honey, can I jump on it sometime?
Yes, I just wanna see
If it's really that expensive kind
You know it balances on your head
Just like a mattress balances
On a bottle of wine
Your brand new leopard-skin pill-box hat

3. Well, if you wanna see the sun rise
Honey, I know where
We'll go out and see it sometime
We'll both just sit there and stare
Me with my belt
Wrapped around my head
And you just sittin' there
In your brand new leopard-skin pill-box hat

4. Well, I asked the doctor if I could see you
It's bad for your health, he said
Yes, I disobeyed his orders
I came to see you
But I found him there instead
You know, I don't mind him cheatin' on me
But I sure wish he'd take that off his head
Your brand new leopard-skin pill-box hat

5. Well, I see you got a new boyfriend
You know, I never seen him before
Well, I saw him
Makin' love to you
You forgot to close the garage door
You might think he loves you for your money
But I know what he really loves you for
It's your brand new leopard-skin pill-box hat

I AND I

WORDS AND MUSIC BY BOB DYLAN

Moderately slow
Am
C
G
1. Been so long since a strange wom-an has slept in my bed.
mf
D
Am
Look how sweet she sleeps, how free must be her dreams.
C
G
In an-oth-er life-time she must have owned the world or been faith-ful-ly wed

Gsus4
D/F♯
Am
To some right - eous king_ who wrote psalms_ be - side moon - lit streams._
Chorus:
A5
G5
D5
I_____ and I___ in cre - a - tion where___ one's na - ture nei - ther
A5
hon - ors nor for - gives. I_____ and I___
G
D
A5
One says to the oth - er, No_____ man sees my face and lives.

1.-4.
5.

Additional Lyrics

2. Think I'll go out and go for a walk.
Not much happenin' here, nothin' ever does.
Besides, if she wakes up now, she'll just want me to talk
I got nothin' to say, 'specially about whatever was.

Chorus

3. Took an untrodden path once, where the swift don't win the race,
It goes the worthy, who can divide the word of truth.
Took a stranger to teach me, to look into justice's beautiful face
And to see an eye for an eye and a tooth for a tooth.

Chorus

5. Noontime, and I'm still pushin' myself along the road, the darkest part,
Into the narrow lanes, I can't stumble or stay put.
Someone else is speakin' with my mouth, but I'm listening only to my heart.
I've made shoes for everyone, even you, while I still go barefoot.

Chorus

4. Outside of two men on a train platform there's nobody in sight,
They're waiting for spring to come, smoking down the track.
The world could come to an end tonight, but that's all right.
She should still be there sleepin' when I get back.

Chorus

MOZAMBIQUE

WORDS AND MUSIC BY BOB DYLAN/JACQUES LEVY

Moderate reggae beat
G/D D A7/D D G/D D A7/D
I like to spend some time in Mo-zam-bique The sun-ny sky is a-
There's lots of pret-ty girls in Mo-zam-bique And plen-ty time for good
mf
D G/D D A7/D D
qua-blue And all the cou-ples danc-ing cheek to cheek.
ro-mance And ev-ery-bod-y likes to stop and speak
C G D C G D
1.
It's ver-y nice to stay a week or two.
To give the spe-cial one you seek a chance Or may-be say hel-lo

2.
Bm
with just a glance. Ly - ing next to her by the o -
F♯m
Em
D
cean Reach-ing out and touch-ing her hand,
Bm
F♯m
G
A
Whis-per-ing your se-cret e - mo - tion Mag - ic in a mag - i - cal land.
G/D
D
A7/D
And when it's time for leav -

D G/D D A7/D D
ing Mo - zam-bique, To say good-bye to sand and sea,
G/D D A7/D D C G D
You turn a - round to take a fi - nal peek And you see why it's so
C G D
u - nique to be A-mong the love - ly peo - ple liv - ing free
C G D
Up - on the beach of sun - ny Mo - zam - bique.

Visions of Johanna

Words and Music by Bob Dylan

Moderately slow
A
D
E7
mf
1. Ain't it just like the night_ to play tricks when you're try - in' to be so
lot where the la - dies play blind - man's bluff with the
lit - tle boy lost,_ he takes him - self so se - ri - ous -
side the mu - se - ums, In - fin - i - ty goes up on
qui - et? We sit here strand - ed, though we're all
key chain And the all - night girls they whis -
ly He brags of his mis - er - y, he likes
tri - al Voic - es ech - o this is what sal -
do - in' our best to de - ny it And Lou -
per of es - ca - pades out on the "D" train We can
to live dan - ger - ous - ly And when
va - tion must be like af - ter a while But Mo - na

E
E7
ise holds a hand-ful of rain, tempt-in' you_ to de -
hear the night watch - man click his flash - light Ask him-self if it's him or them that's real - ly in -
bring - ing her name up He speaks of a fare-well kiss_ to
Li - sa must - a had the high - way blues You can tell_ by the way she
A
D
fy it
sane
me
smiles
Lights flick - er from_ the op - po - site
Lou - ise, she's all right, she's just
He's sure got_ a lot - ta
See the prim - i - tive_ wall - flow - er
A
D
A
loft In this room the heat pipes just cough The
near She's del - i - cate and seems like the mir - ror_ But she just
gall to be so use - less and all Mut - ter -
freeze When the jel - ly - faced wom - en all sneeze Hear the

D
A
coun-try mu - sic sta - tion plays soft But there's noth-ing, real - ly noth-ing to turn
makes it all_ too con-cise and too clear That Jo - han-na's not here
ing small talk_ at the wall while I'm in the
one with_the mus - tache say, "Jeeze, I can't find my knees."
E7
A
off Just Lou-ise and her
The ghost of 'lec - tric - i - ty
hall How can I ex - plain? Oh,
Oh, jewels and bin - oc - u - lars
D
E7
A
lov - er so en - twined And these vi - sions
howls in the bones of her face Where these vi - sions
it's so hard to get on And these vi - sions
hang from the head of the mule But these vi - sions

D
A/C♯
E7
of Jo - han - na that con - quer my mind
of Jo - han - na have now tak - en my place
of Jo - han - na, they kept me up past the dawn
of Jo - han - na, they make it all seem so cruel
A
D
A
mp
1., 2., 3.
4.
A
2. In the emp - ty
3. Now,
4. In -
5. The ped-dler now speaks to the
mf
mf

D E7 A
count - ess who's pre - tend - ing to care for him_ Say - in',
D E7
"Name me some - one that's not a par - a - site and I'll_ go out_ and say_ a prayer_
A E
_ for him" But like Lou - ise_ al - ways says_ "Ya can't
E7 A
look at much,_ can ya man?" As she, her - self, pre - pares for him_

D
A
And Ma - don - na, she still has not showed We see this
D
A
D
emp - ty cage now cor - rode Where her cape of the stage once had
A
D
A
flowed The fid - dler, he now steps to the road He writes
D
A
D
ev - 'ry - thing's been re - turned which was owed On the back of the fish truck that loads
3

A
E7
While my con - science ex - plodes The har -
f
A
D
E
A
mon - i - cas play the skel - e - ton keys and the rain
D
And these vi - sions of Jo - han - na
A/C♯
E7
A
are now all that re - main.